The Science of Living Things

What is Migration?

John Crossingham & Bobbie Kalman

Crabtree Publishing Company

www.crabtreebooks.com

The Science of Living Things Series
A Bobbie Kalman Book

Dedicated by John Crossingham
For Jacq and Terry – because they've got towels

Editor-in-Chief
Bobbie Kalman

Writing team
John Crossingham
Bobbie Kalman

Editors
Amanda Bishop
Kathryn Smithyman
Niki Walker

Computer design
Kymberley McKee Murphy
Margaret Amy Reiach

Production coordinator
Heather Fitzpatrick

Photo researcher
Heather Fitzpatrick

Consultant
Patricia Loesche, PhD., Animal Behavior Program,
Department of Psychology, University of Washington

Photographs
Kenneth J. Howard: page 16 (top)
Wolfgang Kaehler: pages 12, 30
James Kamstra: page 22
Robert McCaw: pages 9 (top), 26, 31
Photo Researchers Inc.: Tom McHugh: page 20
Tom Stack & Associates: Jeff Foott: pages 16 (bottom), 24, 25;
    Mark Newman: page 19;
    Michael S. Nolan: page 17
Other images by Adobe Image Library, Digital Stock,
and Digital Vision

Illustrations
Barbara Bedell: pages 6 (top and bottom right), 16, 27
Patrick Ching: page 6 (center)
Margaret Amy Reiach: pages 24, 25, 26 (right), 28 (bottom), 29
Bonna Rouse: pages 7, 10, 13, 14, 15, 21, 23, 26 (top left),
    28 (top left), 31

Crabtree Publishing Company
www.crabtreebooks.com   1-800-387-7650

PMB 16A
350 Fifth Avenue
Suite 3308
New York, NY
10118

612 Welland Avenue
St. Catharines
Ontario
Canada
L2M 5V6

73 Lime Walk
Headington
Oxford
OX3 7AD
United Kingdom

Cataloging in Publication Data
Crossingham, John
    What is migration? / John Crossingham & Bobbie Kalman.
        p. cm. -- (The science of living things)
        Includes index.
    A presentation of the migratory habits of such animals as geese, eels, frogs and toads and an explanation of how and why animals migrate.
        ISBN 0-86505-988-8 (RLB) -- ISBN 0-86505-965-9 (pbk.)
    1. Animal migration--Juvenile literature. [1. Animals--Migration.] I. Kalman, Bobbie. II. Title. III. Series
    QL754 .C76 2001
    591.56'8--dc21
                                    2001037208

Contents

What is migration?

Most places on Earth have weather changes throughout the year. The temperature may drop, rain may fall nonstop, or rivers may dry up. These changes are called **seasons**. When seasons change, animals must also change to survive. Some grow thicker fur to protect themselves from cold weather. Others hide underground to escape the sun's heat. Many animals simply travel to areas where the weather is better suited to their needs. This journey is called **migration**. By traveling from place to place, migrators stay warm and find food, water, and a safe place to raise their young.

Following instincts

Many animals migrate to the same place year after year. Even animals that have never made the trip before know exactly where to go. Using **instincts,** they follow the migration routes of their ancestors. Instincts are behaviors with which animals are born. Migrating animals have instincts that help them use mountains, stars, and odors as guides on their trip.

Zebra herds are made up of a male, several females, and their foals. Herds migrate over long distances in order to find the proper grasses for feeding.

 # Why leave home?

Animals migrate for many reasons. Winter may be too cold for them to survive. They may run out of food or water in one spot and have to find it in another. Some animals live in one part of the world most of the time, but they travel to another place to mate, or make babies. Animals also migrate at different times. Many birds, for example, migrate twice each year, whereas salmon migrate only twice in a lifetime. Animals such as army ants and wildebeests are almost always on the move from place to place.

The nursery

Sometimes the **habitats**, or homes, of adult animals are too harsh for their babies. Animals such as whales live in cold Arctic waters and then migrate to warmer waters to have their babies. A newborn whale calf does not have a thick layer of **blubber**, or fat, as older whales do. It could not survive in Arctic waters.

Too cold in winter

Some birds and butterflies migrate to escape cold winters that they would not survive. These animals spend summers in the north, and they fly south for the winter. They return to their northern homes in time for spring.

We need food!

Many places in the world have a limited amount of food and water. After eating all the food in one spot, wildebeests and zebras migrate to another place. While they are gone, new plants grow in the areas they left.

Water to land

Some **reptiles**, such as sea turtles and alligators, live in water but lay their eggs on land. **Amphibians** such as frogs do the opposite—they live on land and lay their eggs in water. All these animals migrate to lay their eggs.

Traveling terns

The Arctic tern is the champion of all migrators. It flies over 20,000 miles (32 186 km) a year—that is almost once around the world! The tern nests in the Arctic during the summer. It then flies 11,000 miles (17 700 km) south to spend the winter in Antarctica and South America.

Young terns

Female terns lay eggs as soon as they arrive in the Arctic. During summer in the Arctic, the sun shines almost 24 hours a day. Constant sunshine makes it easy for tern parents to find food for their chicks. The young terns grow quickly and are ready to fly south with their parents by the end of summer.

Follow the coast

The Arctic summer is bright, but it is also short. By August, the terns begin flying south to their other home. Terns fly by following **coastlines**, where the ocean meets the land. To reach Antarctica, some terns fly along the Pacific coastline, and others fly along the Atlantic.

Flying to find food

Terns leave the Arctic to avoid winter.
While it is winter in the Arctic, it is
summer in Antarctica. The sun shines
almost 24 hours a day, just as it did in
the Arctic in summer.

The young terns that have flown to
Antarctica hunt for their own food and
continue to grow. By January or February,
the birds return to the Arctic. They are
now ready to mate and lay eggs.

Canada geese in a "V"

Canada geese are famous migrators. They spend summers in Canada, where they nest and raise their young. In autumn, the young geese fly south with their parents. They fly to the southern United States and Mexico, where winter is much like summer is in Canada.

By migrating, the geese live in mild weather year-round. They travel south in large V-shaped flocks.

Flying in a V formation helps the birds save energy on their long journey. Other birds such as snow geese and sandhill cranes also fly in a V-formation.

Flying together

When birds fly in a V-formation, the bird at the front of the "V" flaps its wings and leaves a disturbance called a **wake** in the air. A wake is like the series of small waves a motorboat leaves in the water. The wake left by the bird at the front spreads out in a V-shape behind the bird. The other birds line up along the "V" behind the leader. Each bird in the line adds to the wake. Flying in the wake is easier than flying up front, so the birds at the end of the "V" do not have to flap their wings as hard as the birds ahead of them. The geese take turns being at the front so none of the birds will become too tired and the group can move quickly.

Map of the world

Canada geese do not fly along coastlines when they migrate. Doing so would take too long. Instead, they fly over the mainland. They use **landmarks** such as mountains and rivers to guide them on their way.

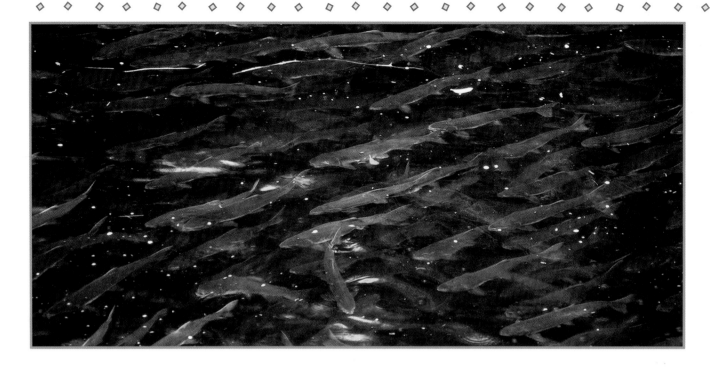

Salmon swim to spawn

Few aquatic animals can survive in both salt water and fresh water, but Atlantic and Pacific salmon can. Salmon begin their lives in calm freshwater streams. After two years, they migrate over 1,000 miles (1 600 km) from their freshwater homes to the oceans. For the next four years, the salmon live and hunt in salt water. They grow into adults in the ocean, and at the end of their lives, they return to the stream where they were born. There, the adults **spawn**, or lay eggs. Soon afterward, they die.

A fresh start

A female salmon lays thousands of eggs at a time. The **alevins**, or babies, are only a few inches long when they hatch. Many are eaten, but some survive for the next stage of their journey.

Out to the ocean

When the salmon are two to three years old, they follow the stream's **current**, which is the natural flow of water toward the ocean. The stream leads them to wide, fast-flowing rivers. The salmon follow these rivers to the ocean.

Upstream battle

After four years in the ocean, the salmon make the difficult trip back to their home in the stream. When the salmon were young, the river currents helped carry them toward the ocean. To return to their **spawning grounds**, or places where they hatched, the salmon must swim great distances against the powerful currents.

An adult salmon is a strong fish. Its strength helps it fight its way back to the stream in which it hatched. On its way, it often has to leap over rocks in the water. A grizzly might be waiting to catch it!

yolk sac

*A newly-hatched salmon feeds off its **yolk sac** for about a month. The yolk sac provides the baby with all the **nutrients** it needs to grow. When the yolk sac is used up, the baby is called a **parr**.*

Eels on the move

European eels migrate from salt water to fresh water. The eels begin their lives in the saltwater Sargasso Sea, which is part of the Atlantic Ocean near the equator. They then migrate across the Atlantic to Europe's freshwater lakes and streams, where they live as adults. When they are ready to mate, the eels return to the spawning ground to lay their eggs.

When the female eels arrive at the spawning ground, they dive down 1,000 feet (305 m) to the sea floor. There they lay thousands of eggs. The eggs hatch into tiny **larvas**, or babies. The larvas are each less than one inch long, and they look like **transparent**, or clear, leaves.

Growing up on the move

Unlike young salmon, the eel larvas migrate almost immediately after they hatch. They are not very strong, but ocean currents help carry them to their new home. This journey takes three years. Along the way, the larvas slowly grow into the second stage of their lives. They are now called **elvers**. By the time the elvers reach Europe, they look like adult eels, but they are only three inches (7.5 cm) long.

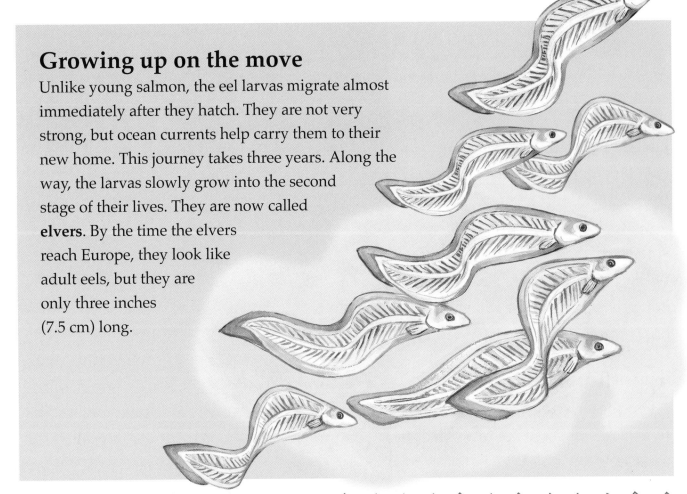

Going separate ways

Adult females swim **upriver** against the current to live in freshwater ponds and streams. The male eels, however, stay in the salt water. They live and feed in bays along the ocean's edge. Scientists are not sure why the males and females split up.

Together again

After a few years, the female eels return to the ocean. They reunite with the male eels, and together they migrate over 1,000 miles (1 600 km) to the Sargasso Sea. Males **fertilize** the eggs of the females, which will soon hatch into new eel larvas.

North American cousins

North American eels make a journey similar to that of European eels, but their trip takes only eighteen months. North American eels are also born in the Sargasso Sea, but instead of heading for Europe, the larvas swim to the coasts of Maine and eastern Canada.

 # Go, gray whales!

When gray whales travel long distances, a calf usually swims just above its mother. She gently nudges the baby to the surface to teach it to breathe.

*Whales rest one **hemisphere,** or half, of their brain while the other half keeps the whale going. During migration, the whales stop only for short rests.*

Gray whales spend the summer in the northern Pacific Ocean. At the end of summer, the giant sea mammals migrate south to warmer waters. There, they give birth to **calves** and raise them.

Food for all

Gray whales are **baleen** whales. They have long strips of bone called baleen inside their mouths. The whales feed by using their baleen to strain tiny animals called **krill** from the water. In summer, the northern Pacific Ocean is full of krill. A gray whale eats more than a ton of krill every day! It eats a lot to form a thick coat of blubber. Blubber keeps the whale warm.

Going back to Baja

By late summer, krill have become scarce, and the weather grows colder. The whales start a 5,000 mile (8 047 km) migration south. Their journey ends off the coast of Baja, California in Mexico. The whales do not feed during the winter—they live off the body fat they stored in the summer.

Mating season

Pregnant female whales are the first whales to make the journey to Baja. They arrive in December and give birth to their calves. A calf feeds only on its mother's milk. The other gray whales arrive in January to mate.

Females that become pregnant will not give birth until the following December. By April, the whales begin migrating north again. While they were gone, more krill were born. There is once again plenty of food for the whales and their calves.

*To see where it is going, a gray whale sometimes **spyhops**, or lifts its head out of the water.*

Wildebeests in motion

Wildebeests are hoofed mammals that live in large herds on the African **savannah**. The savannah is a very dry area of land. Animals that live there often have difficulty finding enough water and fresh grass. Wildebeests constantly migrate in search of food.

Whenever necessary

Wildebeests do not migrate at set times. Rather than once or twice a year, they move when water or food becomes scarce.

Sometimes a herd needs to travel only a few miles to find fresh grasses. In dry weather, however, the journey can take much longer.

Helping hand

The weather is often so hot that rivers dry up, and there is no water to drink. Wildebeests are sometimes saved by another African migrator—the elephant. Elephants use their **tusks** to dig into the mud and reach water that is underground.

Caribou journeys

Caribou live in Canada and Alaska, but they migrate in search of food just as wildebeests do. They spend winters near the edge of northern forests where the trees provide shelter and some food. In spring, caribou migrate north to the **tundra**. Caribou herds feed on the mosses and lichens that grow on the tundra in summer.

Well-worn trails

Caribou have used the same migration trails for hundreds of years. The trails are well-worn from the hoofprints of thousands of caribou.

Caribou migrate in two groups. The **cows**, or females, leave first. Along the way, pregnant cows give birth to calves, which are able to walk an hour after they are born. They continue migrating with their mothers. In a few weeks, the **bulls**, or males, follow the females.

Swim for it

When migrating caribou reach a river, the herd jumps in and swims across. Some caribou drown, but most complete the journey. Caribou are excellent swimmers. They cross rivers and even small lakes when migrating.

Caribou are hunted by wolves, so they travel in herds for protection.

Lemmings on the run

Lemmings are small mouselike rodents that live in the northern parts of North America, Europe, and Asia. Lemmings usually stay in one area, but during some years, their population grows too large and huge groups of lemmings must leave to find new homes. This mass migration is called an **emigration**. An emigration is a one-way trip from one place to another. It takes place when food, water, or space runs out.

A natural balance

Lemmings give birth to **litters**, or large groups of young. The babies grow quickly and soon have their own litters. Even though lemmings are born often and in large numbers, they are eaten by many **predators**, including owls, wolves, hawks, and foxes. The predators eat so many lemmings that they usually prevent the population from growing too large.

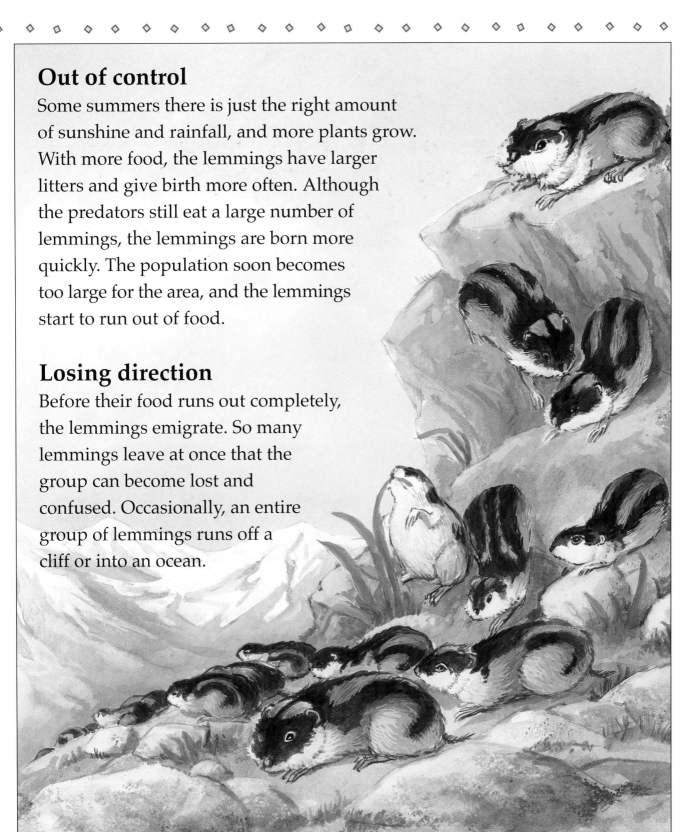

Out of control

Some summers there is just the right amount of sunshine and rainfall, and more plants grow. With more food, the lemmings have larger litters and give birth more often. Although the predators still eat a large number of lemmings, the lemmings are born more quickly. The population soon becomes too large for the area, and the lemmings start to run out of food.

Losing direction

Before their food runs out completely, the lemmings emigrate. So many lemmings leave at once that the group can become lost and confused. Occasionally, an entire group of lemmings runs off a cliff or into an ocean.

Marching army ants

Army ants live in South America, and they are always on the move. Scientists call these constant travelers **nomads**. Army ants march at night across the forest floor in huge groups. They cover the ground like a massive blanket of insects! As they march, the ants attack and eat almost anything they meet.

Why keep going?

Scientists are not sure why army ants migrate. The weather does not change much from place to place. There is plenty of food—the ants often leave behind leftovers when they march to a new location. Some scientists suggest that the ants march so they will avoid running out of food for themselves and their young.

Building a bridge

Army ants meet many obstacles during their travels. Instead of going around small gaps between leaves, the ants build bridges using their own bodies. One ant stands at the edge of a leaf, and another climbs on top of it and ventures out a little farther. The ants continue climbing onto one another until they are linked to form a bridge.

Keep the queen dry!

A group of ants is called a **colony**. The queen is the largest and most important member of the colony. She is the only ant that can lay eggs. When army ants come to a stream, they gather around the queen to form a ball. This ball acts as a raft to float the queen across. The ants take turns climbing to the top of the ball so that very few will drown in the stream.

Halt!

The army ants march every night for two to three weeks. They then **camp**, or rest, for three weeks. While they camp, the queen lays thousands of eggs that hatch into legless larvas. When the ants march again, **nurse ants** carry the larvas on their backs. At their next stop, they will place these larvas inside **cocoons** to grow.

By the time the colony is ready to move again, the larvas will have grown into adult ants. They are now ready to march with the rest of the colony.

Migrating monarchs

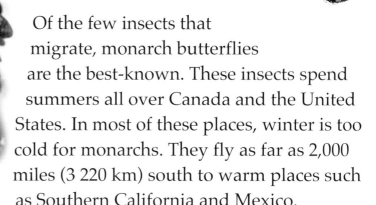

Of the few insects that migrate, monarch butterflies are the best-known. These insects spend summers all over Canada and the United States. In most of these places, winter is too cold for monarchs. They fly as far as 2,000 miles (3 220 km) south to warm places such as Southern California and Mexico.

The butterfly tree

Like migrating birds, monarchs leave their summer homes in early autumn. Millions of monarchs form large flocks that migrate together. When they reach California and Mexico, they do not feed or lay new eggs. Instead, they rest on trees. Thousands of monarchs gather on the branches of each tree. There are so many butterflies that they look like leaves on the tree.

The monarchs do not move around much after they land. They **hibernate**, or sleep very deeply. Their body temperatures drop, and their hearts beat more slowly. The monarchs wake up in spring, ready to fly north.

Carry on without me

On the return trip, some butterflies stop to mate. The females then lay eggs. The butterflies usually die shortly after mating. Their eggs hatch, however, and grow into new butterflies that continue the trip their parents started. No matter where they were born, the butterflies know to continue north and then to fly south when autumn begins.

Back to the pond

Amphibians are animals that live underwater for the first part of their lives and then live on land as adults. Frogs and toads are amphibians. They grow from eggs hatched in a pond, called a breeding pond. Most frogs and toads stay near their breeding ponds their entire lives, but some do not. Many live in woods or other areas away from the pond. Each spring, these frogs and toads migrate back to the pond to breed. They find their way by instinct.

A short challenge

Frogs and toads do not migrate very far. Their homes are usually within a few miles of the pond, but even a mile can be a challenging journey for a small frog!

Part of the life cycle

Migrations are part of an amphibian **life cycle**. A life cycle is the set of changes all animals go through from the time they are born or hatch until they become adults. Amphibians begin life as tadpoles swimming in breeding ponds. Their bodies change completely as they grow legs and lungs. As adults, they leave the pond and live on land. When they are ready, they migrate back to the pond again.

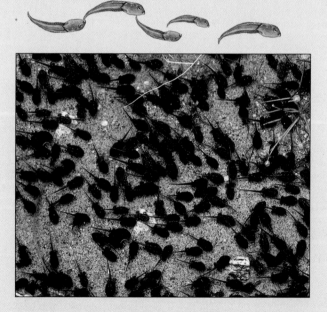

These tadpoles will return to this pond to breed when they are fully grown toads.

'Gators to land

Alligators are **reptiles**. They migrate to breed, just as amphibians do. Unlike amphibians, however, alligators are born on land and live most of their adult lives in the water. Alligators live in rivers and shallow coastal waters. When it is time to mate each spring, they migrate onto land. A female alligator searches for a sheltered area and lays her eggs. Unlike most frogs and toads, which leave their young, alligator mothers raise their babies.

Alligators are not fully grown until they are more than six years old.

Sea turtles swim home

Like alligators, sea turtles are reptiles that live in the water but lay their eggs on land. The turtles migrate much farther than alligators do, however. Some sea turtles migrate over 1,500 miles (2 415 km) to lay their eggs.

Adult sea turtles live in warm parts of the open ocean, but they began life on a beach hundreds of miles away. Despite the great distance, sea turtles return to the beach on which they hatched to lay eggs of their own. Some scientists think the turtles find their way by following certain scents. Others suggest that sea turtles use the sun and stars as guides, just as ancient sailors did.

Sea turtles mate at sea. Females lay their eggs on land, but male sea turtles never leave the water.

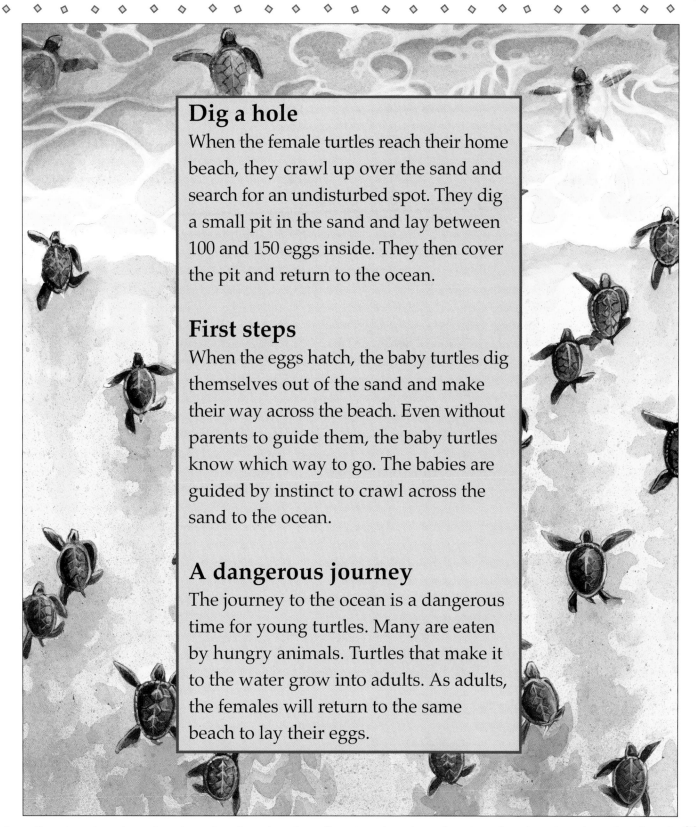

Dig a hole

When the female turtles reach their home beach, they crawl up over the sand and search for an undisturbed spot. They dig a small pit in the sand and lay between 100 and 150 eggs inside. They then cover the pit and return to the ocean.

First steps

When the eggs hatch, the baby turtles dig themselves out of the sand and make their way across the beach. Even without parents to guide them, the baby turtles know which way to go. The babies are guided by instinct to crawl across the sand to the ocean.

A dangerous journey

The journey to the ocean is a dangerous time for young turtles. Many are eaten by hungry animals. Turtles that make it to the water grow into adults. As adults, the females will return to the same beach to lay their eggs.

Keeping track

How do scientists know so much about migration? They have many tools to help them track animals. The tools range from simple metal tags to complex radio **transmitters** that send signals to satellites. Tags and transmitters allow scientists to recognize and track an animal without disturbing it.

Bands and tags

One of the simplest ways to mark an animal is with a band or a tag. Scientists can wrap metal bands around the thin legs of birds. They can attach tags to an animal's ears or tail. Each band and tag has a serial number and other information that the scientists record. Scientists also write down where and when the tagged animal was seen.

When the animal shows up in another area, scientists can read its tag to learn the location of the animal's home. If you find an injured or dead animal that has been tagged, ask an adult to call the number printed on the tag. Never approach an injured animal yourself!

This scientist has wrapped a metal band around a bird's leg to keep track of its travels.

Blips on the screen

Scientists also use **radar** signals to count animals in migrating flocks and herds. Radar equipment sends **soundwaves** toward the animals. When a soundwave hits an animal's transmitter, it bounces back to the radar dish. By recording the signals that return, scientists can count the number of tagged animals in a specific area. Scientists then **estimate** the actual number of animals in that area.

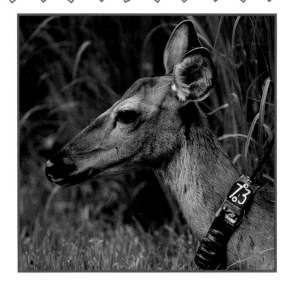

Tune into my station

Scientists also use radio transmitters to track animal movements. Instead of a tag, the animal is fitted with a collar that has a small transmitter on it. The transmitter sends radio signals up to satellites in space. The satellites then send the signals to equipment in scientific labs and field stations. Scientists read the signals to follow the animal's movements.

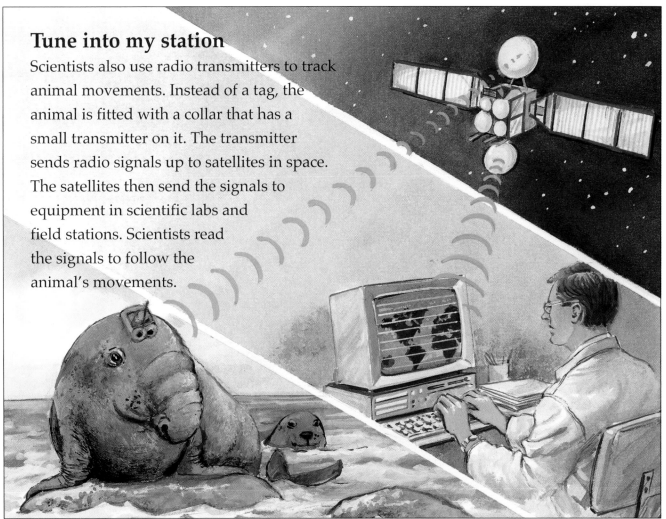

Glossary

alevin A young salmon after it has hatched from its egg

aquatic Describing an animal that lives in the water

baleen Thin, bony plates in the mouths of some whales used to strain food from water

coastline The line along the seashore, where the ocean meets the land

current The direction in which water flows in a river or ocean

emigration A one-way journey made by an animal to find a new home

energy The power needed to do things

hibernation An animal's winter sleep during which its heartbeat and breathing slow down and its body temperature drops to near freezing

instinct A natural awareness or "knowledge" that controls animal behaviors such as mating and migration

larva A young animal, especially an insect or fish, after it has hatched from its egg

nomad An animal that often wanders from place to place

nutrient A natural substance needed by a body to grow and stay healthy

predator An animal that hunts and eats other animals

radar Equipment that sends and receives soundwaves to reflect the shapes of objects in their path

spawn To lay eggs

tundra A cold, treeless region in the Arctic with very little vegetation

Index

1 2 3 4 5 6 7 8 9 0   Printed in the U.S.A.   1 0 9 8 7 6 5 4 3 2

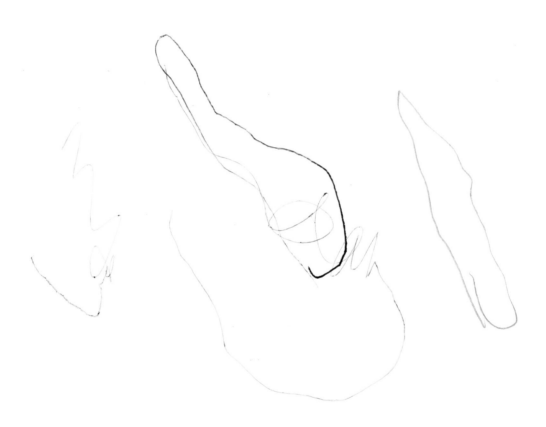